Congregations as
Learning
Communities
Tools for Shaping Your Future

Dennis G. Campbell

An Alban Institute Publication

Copyright © 2000 by the Alban Institute. All rights reserved.

This material may not be photocopied or reproduced in any way without written permission.

Library of Congress Card Number 00-104848

ISBN 1-56699-237-0

CONTENTS

99958

ACKNOWLEDGMENTS

I would like to thank my colleagues at the University of the South, School of Theology Seminary and Programs Center, the Church Development Institute, and the Alban Institute for their assistance in the development of this book. The initial research for this work was a project for the School of Theology Advanced Degrees Program. Thanks to Mr. and Mrs. Ed Pratt for the use of a house and Mrs. Margarett Vandiver for an apartment where the initial draft and later revised manuscript were written. Thanks also to my wife and colleague, Peggy Bosmyer, and our four children, Michael, Larnie, Mary Hannah, and Caitlin. Finally, a special thanks to Jean Caffey Lyles for her editorial skill and patience and Beth Ann Gaede who gently inquired, nudged, and coached me through this entire process.

CHAPTER 1

Learning Communities and Oversight

The world we live in is so complex and changing so rapidly that most of us feel overwhelmed with the challenges before us. Nowhere is this state of mind more prevalent than in congregational life. Once the local church was a haven of calm stability. But now that our external context is constantly in flux, congregational stability may not be attainable, and possibly not even desirable.

Peter Senge, author of *The Fifth Discipline:The Art and Practice of the Learning Organization* and senior lecturer in organizational behavior science at the Massachusetts Institute of Technology, argues that the future of every organization depends on its ability to learn together as a community.[1] I agree with Senge and would add that in our rapidly evolving religious scene, congregations that seek only to achieve some degree of stability, rather than constantly opening themselves to learning and responding to external and internal change, will surely die or, at best, exist at a marginal level with little mission or ministry.

The time is past when we needed only periodically to initiate redevelopment efforts in a congregation, attain a level of new vitality and health, and then settle back and relax until the time came to do it all over. The healthy congregations of the 21st century will be those that leave that process of linear thinking behind and create within their internal culture the behavioral patterns, structures, and values that will naturally position them for a continual cycle of redevelopment. These congregations will never be finished with their learning, but they will recognize that the only healthy and faithful response to a rapidly changing culture and environment is continually to ask what God is calling them to do, and what they must learn or unlearn to respond faithfully to that call.

Changing the internal cultural and systemic DNA of a congregation to create a learning community will require the ultimate transforming effort. The transformation cannot be just a new program or organizational structure for the congregation. Change must be instituted at a deep enough level of the congregation's corporate life that eventually the new learning is absorbed without anyone's conscious thought.

Developing a learning community is not an experience with a distinct beginning and ending. A congregation will develop into a learning community as it perpetually uses a set of tools and disciplines that enables it to remain open to what God is calling it to be.

The term "learning organization" first cropped up in scholarly publications on organizational behavior and organizational development; it emerged in popular literature through Senge's book *The Fifth Discipline*. Before Senge's book was published in 1990, one could read about learning-organization theory in academic journals; but the theory was not easily accessible and was difficult to apply. Senge describes his inspiration for the book in the introduction to the paperback edition:

> The vision that became *The Fifth Discipline* was born one morning in the fall of 1987. During my meditation that morning, I suddenly became aware that "the learning organization" would likely become a new management fad. Having watched similar fads (such as "creating shared visions") develop in the past, I knew that the work being done at MIT, Innovation Associates and by colleagues elsewhere represented a unique body of practical knowledge that could contribute to organizational learning. I also realized that if we were to influence the fad, we needed to "put a stake in the ground"—to establish a position concerning what was possible, a position that would become a point of reference as the fad cycle developed.[2]

Senge's candor in acknowledging the concept of "the learning organization" as a fad is refreshing. The church experiences its share of fads.

We tend to latch onto new approaches, programs, and methods as if they were the Gospel itself, and then within a year we are promoting some other innovative tool as the real thing. It is important to recognize that the various approaches and tools we use in congregational ministry run a life cycle of popularity. Whether any approach remains in long-term practice depends on whether it is rooted in and consistent with Christian theology and identity. It is my hope that the tools I describe in this work will be helpful and effective, but I offer them with the realistic understanding that they may not be useful to every congregation.

Since publication of Senge's book, as people have come to realize the importance of community to organizational learning, Senge and others have adopted the expression "learning community" in place of "learning organization." The former is the term I will use in adapting for congregations the tools that Senge and others have created.

Encapsulating a foundational understanding of learning communities, Senge describes five disciplines: systems thinking, personal mastery, mental models, the building of shared vision, and team learning. Congregational leaders who want to help their faith communities become learning communities need to understand these disciplines.

SYSTEMS THINKING

Systems thinking, the primary discipline, serves as the "cornerstone that underlies all five disciplines."[3] One way of describing systems *thinking* is that it is the practical application of systems *theory*. General systems theory emerged a half-century ago and has been applied to a variety of disciplines, from biology to psychotherapy. In the church our initial use of systems theory was built on psychologist Rabbi Edwin Friedman's application of family systems therapy to congregations in his book *Generation to Generation*. Peter Steinke and others have further developed this approach.

A direct application of general systems theory is found in the work of Paul Dietrich, director of the Center for Parish Development in Chicago. Dietrich and his colleagues have developed an elaborate systems model for analyzing a congregation. Dietrich's model provides a snapshot of the overall congregational system and its subsystems.

Jay Forrester, professor at MIT, is the true pioneer of systems thinking. He strove to understand the dynamic complexity of systems from the inside out and created a field called "systems dynamics," which fostered many of the systems-thinking tools used today. These tools are used to look beneath the events and forces of a system to discover the complex and subtle structures that affect or influence specific behaviors. Many of the advanced tools that Forrester created require an extensive mathematical background to appreciate and use intricate computer modeling. However, the tools we will use are accessible to anyone with the desire and the discipline to learn, practice, and apply them.

Senge describes systems thinking as a conceptual framework, a body of knowledge and tools developed to make the full range of behavioral patterns of an organization clearer, and consequently to reveal the high leverage points for effective change. These leverage points include procedures, processes, people, and structures that have a significant effect on the larger system.[4] By implementing small change at these leverage points, one can initiate larger change in the overall system.

PERSONAL MASTERY

According to Senge, personal mastery is

> the discipline of personal growth and learning. People with high levels of personal mastery are continually expanding their ability to create the results in life they truly seek. From their quest for continual learning comes the spirit of the learning organization.[5]

Senge explains that although personal mastery is grounded in competence and skills and requires spiritual growth, it goes beyond competence and skills. He describes personal mastery as "approaching one's life as a creative work, living life from a creative as opposed to a reactive viewpoint."

Personal mastery applied in a Christian context would be similar to the Benedictine vow of conversion of life, which author and lecturer Esther de Waal describes as "obedience and perseverance to the lifelong process of being transformed as one follows Christ."[6] De Waal is describing what most of us would call the process of sanctification, the theological concept that God is continually working with us to transform us into whole persons. Senge describes this kind of commitment to individual growth as the spiritual foundation of a learning community. He asserts that an "organization's commitment to and capacity for learning can be no greater than that of its members."[7]

It is important to understand the necessity for a balanced relationship between individual learning and corporate, organizational learning. The creative tension between the two is a healthy polarity that requires balance but generates creative life. The community needs to learn together as a body, but individuals within the community need to learn in their respective areas of interest and concern. It is similar to the understanding that Christians need to practice individual times of prayer and devotion—but the community needs also to gather and practice some form of corporate worship. There is an absolute necessity for both if one is to live a healthy, productive Christian life.

The other polarity in personal mastery is the tension between the task of continually envisioning and clarifying what we recognize as important and what we see as our current reality. We can imagine and sometimes even see ourselves as perfected, whole humans, but this image lives in tension with the reality of our sinful human nature. In one sense, Senge is describing Paul's dilemma, but possibly in a more positive light. Senge sees this tension as the source of a generative creativity. He argues that it is the difference between these two poles—vision and reality—that gives rise to the creative tension that can draw us into the ultimate vision of what we are capable of becoming. Senge describes this creative dynamic:

> The juxtaposition of vision (what we want) and a clear picture of current reality (where we are relative to what we want) generates what we call "creative tension"; a force to bring them together, caused by the natural tendency of tension to seek resolution. The essence of personal mastery is learning how to generate and sustain creative tension in our lives.[8]

MENTAL MODELS

Senge describes mental models as "deeply ingrained assumptions, generalizations, or even pictures or images that influence how we understand the world and how we take action."[9] Mental models are developed in a congregation through corporate experiences and often as a result of the congregation's learning to manage a particular challenge or problem.

These deep-seated models affect our thinking and consequently our actions at an invisible, subconscious level. Senge describes working with mental models as if we were to turn a mirror inward to unearth the internal pictures that each of us uses to understand the world—and in our case, the life of our congregations. We critically scrutinize these internal pictures, which shape how we think and behave. People expose these models of thinking in a trusted community and allow them to be influenced by others.

Mental models do not jump up and say, "Here we are!" They are surfaced intentionally through the process of dialogue rather than mere discussion. By dialogue I mean a level of communication at which people are able temporarily to suspend their judgment about an issue and listen intently to one another, instead of merely batting opinions back and forth. Often the answers to our problems are right in front of us, but we are unable to see them because of our mental models. Small congregations often suffer from mental models that are a product of large-church thinking. These congregations sometimes suffer low self-esteem and feelings of inadequacy because their mental models say that to be a "real" church, they must have a 40-voice choir, a graded Christian education program, and an extensive committee structure—all of which is impossible with only 30 people in church on Sunday.

Our mental models often block us from being able to do what God is calling us to do; they prevent us from seeing the resources that we have and the skills we possess. Initially, Moses suffered from a mental model that said one must be an articulate, eloquent speaker to lead people.

BUILDING SHARED VISION

There is so much talk about "shared vision" today that we have reduced the concept almost to a cliché, and yet when the authentic phenomenon somehow appears, we are once again reminded of the absolute necessity for vision in our congregational as well as individual lives. We have examined our vision nearly to the point that people flinch when they hear the word. Many congregations have been subjected to vision-statement processes that have resulted in 30-page documents bound and appropriately stashed in the back section of a filing cabinet. With the expected task of completing a vision statement fulfilled, the congregation returns to business as usual.

This energy-depleting experience is not what Senge means by building a shared vision. My favorite example of a shared vision is the one Senge offers from a movie:

> You may remember the movie Spartacus, an adaptation of the story of a Roman gladiator/slave who led an army of slaves in an uprising conquered by the general Marcus Crassus after a long siege and battle. In the movie, Crassus tells the thousand survivors in Spartacus's army, "You have been slaves. You will be slaves again. But you will be spared your rightful punishment of crucifixion by the mercy of the Roman legions. All you need to do is turn over to me the slave Spartacus, because we do not know him by sight."
>
> After a long pause, Spartacus (played by Kirk Douglas) stands up and says, "I am Spartacus." Then the man next to him stands up and says, "I am Spartacus." The next man stands up and also says, "No, I am Spartacus." Within a minute, everyone in the army is on his feet.
>
> It does not matter whether this story is apocryphal or not; it demonstrates a deep truth. Each man, by standing up, chose death. But the loyalty of Spartacus's army was not to Spartacus the man. Their loyalty was to a shared vision which Spartacus had inspired—the idea that they could be free men. This vision was so compelling that no man could bear to give it up and return to slavery.[10]

This kind of vision is not generated through a laborious step-by-step process with the vestry on a weekend retreat and condensed into a statement printed on the placemats at the "Vision Celebration Dinner." This shared vision emerges from the individual hearts and souls of people who have lived life and suffered and yet dare to risk struggling with the Holy Spirit to imagine the astounding tomorrow to which God is calling the congregation. This vision is a vulnerable work of art that arises from a people who dare to ask, "Is anything too wonderful for God?"

Again Senge puts it well:

> A shared vision is not an idea. It is not even an important idea such as freedom. It is rather, a force in people's hearts, a force of impressive power. It may be inspired by an idea, but once it goes further—if it is compelling enough to acquire the support of more

than one person—then it is no longer an abstraction. It is palpable. People begin to see it as if it exists. Few, if any, forces in human affairs are as powerful as shared vision.[11]

Senge argues that shared vision is important because it provides the focus and energy for learning, and it is the ability to learn that will move a congregation forward into a new day. Shared visions are never finished and complete; they are always being revised and recreated because they are alive and organic. Tools and processes can be helpful, but they are only means to an end. A true shared vision is co-created with the Holy Spirit and always involves people's hearts and prayerful discernment.

TEAM LEARNING

Most of us at one time or another have had the experience of working with an excellent team of people who complemented each other's strengths and compensated for one another's weaknesses in such a way that it seemed we could do almost anything. What Senge means by "team" is a group of people who have developed a level of trust, cooperation, and coordination that enables the group, by combining efforts, skills, and knowledge, to experience a cumulative level of intelligence and productivity that exceeds the sum of group members' individual efforts.

Many of us experience this phenomenon on the athletic field, one of the few places in our individualistic society for us to support one another in our respective roles for a common purpose. Senge offers an excellent example of basketball star Bill Russell explaining his experience with the Boston Celtics:

By design and by talent, we were a team of specialists, and like a team of specialists in any field, our performance depended both on individual excellence and how well we worked together. None of us had to strain to understand that we had to complement each others' specialties; it was simply a fact, and we all tried to figure out ways to make our combination more effective. Off the court, most of us were oddballs by society's standards—not the kind of people who blend in with others or who tailor their personalities to match what's expected of them.

Every so often a Celtic game would heat up so that it became more than a physical or even mental game and would be magical. The feeling is difficult to describe and I certainly never talked about it when I was playing. When it happened I could feel my play rise to a new level. . . . It would surround not only me and the other Celtics but also the players on the other team, and even the referees. . . . At that special level, all sorts of odd things happened. The game would be in the white heat of competition, and yet I wouldn't feel competitive, which is a miracle in itself. . . . The game would move so fast that every fake, cut, and pass would be surprising, and yet nothing could surprise me. It was almost as if we were playing in slow motion. During those spells, I could most sense how the next play would develop and where the next shot would be taken.[12]

Senge asserts that the key to this synergistic teamwork is a community aligned; working for a common, committed purpose; going in the same direction toward a shared vision. "Individuals do not sacrifice their personal interests to the larger team vision; rather, the shared vision becomes an extension of their personal visions."[13] Senge also warns against the danger of empowering an unaligned community, because its energy worsens chaos— for example, a group of people that becomes a mob.

Communities that achieve this level of alignment and teamwork are able not only to accomplish synergistically more than their sum parts, but also to integrate knowledge and skill at a much higher level. Oh, for the day that a church council could function with the teamwork that Russell identifies in the Boston Celtics!

OVERSIGHT AND SYSTEMS THINKING

All the disciplines are important and function interdynamically, and there are no sure and certain rules or procedures as to which discipline to consider first. The overarching discipline is systems thinking, which requires a nonlinear approach to implementing the other disciplines and is an essential tool in the ministry of oversight carried out by lay and clergy leadership.

A clear understanding of the ministry of oversight is one of the primary characteristics of a congregation that wishes to become a learning community. The concept of oversight is rooted in the Greek biblical word *episcopé*, which means to oversee. Certainly, some are called to special, focused ministries, but there must always be a group consisting of clergy and laity that exercises the responsibility of overseeing the whole. In various polities and traditions, the language and organizational structures may differ, but the ministry is essentially the same, to oversee the ministry of the whole, the big picture of the local congregational expression of the church.

I have a friend who says she resents the word "oversight" because it is just a churchy term for management. She argues that we should get comfortable and honest about the need for management in our congregations. I disagree. I am all for recognizing the need for responsible management in congregations, but the word oversight implies and includes more than institutional management. Oversight means consistently viewing the congregation as an organic being; it includes the much-needed day-to-day management and administration, but it also includes the leadership necessary to develop and articulate the vision and mission of a congregation. It is also leadership's responsibility, when necessary, to shape and change the internal culture and structure of a congregation in response to that vision and mission. Oversight is a much larger systemic task than mere management and administration. And this broader understanding of oversight is a minimal prerequisite for developing a learning community.

Today, more than ever, clergy are confused as to their role. Some innovative approaches to ministry are compartmentally and mechanistically dividing and redistributing the functions of the ordained ministry as if it too were just another machine. Many clergy have been trained to be the primary, professional ministers in their congregations, but what we desperately need today are clergy who will oversee ministry in partnership with laity. The church needs teams of clergy and laity who will consistently and effectively recruit, train, and empower people to carry out the ministry of the church in the community beyond the Sunday worship service.

Teaching an adult class on ministry, I once asked class members to tell me what they thought my functions should be as their parish priest. The list was long, and I was feeling overwhelmed just writing down all their expectations. Finally, as I began the fourth page of newsprint, some wonderful saint raised his hand and said, "Wait a minute. It would be impossible for you to do everything we've got listed up there." And I replied, "Yes, it is impossible, and that is why we need everyone to minister. I can't even oversee all of this ministry alone. That's why there have to be some of you who are willing to serve as leaders and share that responsibility."

It was a pivotal moment in our life together when, as a congregation, we learned a new understanding of what ministry can and should be. Those of us who serve on administrative boards, sessions, vestries, councils, and long-range planning teams, whether as clergy or laity, have been called out from our respective, specialized ministries to serve in a ministry of the whole. Our love and passion may be for music or education or outreach or whatever, but if we are called to serve in the ministry of oversight, we are asked to set those special interests aside and to broaden our focus to the entire body.

Clergy almost always have specific areas of strength or interest, such as preaching, liturgy, pastoral counseling, or teaching. These areas must also be kept in balance and perspective if clergy are to share effectively in the ministry of oversight. I suspect that the primary activity that entices clergy away from oversight ministry is the temptation to run around putting out small brushfires of discontent in the congregation. Clergy spend an inordinate amount of time trying to make people happy; this demanding task uses vast amounts of energy.

A problem I encounter repeatedly when working with congregations or judicatories is the perception of people in leadership positions that they are serving in representative roles as advocates for their respective special interests. The typical dedicated lay leader insists, "I am the person on the administrative board who is here to make sure the choir [Sunday school, outreach ministry] gets a fair shake." Rare is the leader who understands that she is there to oversee all of those ministries—not just on a singular, compartmental basis, but with a view large enough to encompass how those ministries interact and affect one another and the congregation as a whole.

The judicatory's version of this problem is experienced when the Christian education commission does not realize that some of its objectives are being supported by other groups such as the youth ministry department, and that cooperation between the two entities would be mutually beneficial. Sometimes those responsible for managing the financial resources of the diocese become so focused on their task that they become disconnected from the mission of the church and instead see their purpose only as protecting the money.

The apostle Paul said that we are the body of Christ, so we who serve in the ministry of oversight cannot be concerned simply with the hand or the foot but with the whole body. Seeing the whole is probably even more of a challenge today than it was in Paul's time, because we are products of a rational, Western, analytical culture that says the best way to understand anything is to take it apart piece by piece.

When I was a child, I loved to take things apart—clocks, bicycles, radios, anything. I took them apart because I wanted to understand them, to see how they worked. Surrounded by the various pieces, I rarely came to an understanding of how the radio or clock worked, and unfortunately I usually could not get the pieces back together.

Understanding a congregation has more to do with what is going on dynamically between the parts than it does with the parts themselves. We can understand a congregation when we come to understand the dynamic relationships between its parts. Our temptation is to focus on one aspect of a congregation. Many a newly ordained person has spent an enormous amount of time and energy studying the content of the congregation's various programs, ministries, and even personalities, only to remain confused as to what makes this place behave the way it does. Understanding a congregation requires that we persevere beyond this initial examination of the content of the parts. The real challenge is to identify how these parts dynamically affect and interact with one another—a mysterious and arduous task.

Not only does oversight involve seeing the various parts and how they interrelate; it also requires keeping in sight the history of what has gone on before in the congregation, as well as daring to look into the future to anticipate what waits around the corner in the years to come. Often the missing pieces of the congregational puzzle lie in incidents almost forgotten but still deeply embedded in the system and internal culture and still subtly affecting behavioral patterns.

The ministry of oversight also requires thinking and acting strategically. Why are we doing whatever we are doing? Why are we doing it this way? Does our activity have anything to do with our purpose as a congregation or diocese? We who serve in the ministry of oversight are the ones responsible for whether a congregation worships stability to the point of idolatry and stagnation, or whether it is willing to risk following God into new promised lands of ministry and service.

The challenging task of oversight requires a variety of gifts and talents that not everyone possesses. Even those who have the potential for oversight need tools and practice to realize and develop their ministry. Strong oversight by a team of clergy and laity is a minimal prerequisite for developing congregations as learning communities. At the same time, learning communities are the ideal context for people with the potential to develop fully as strong ministers of oversight.

TOOLS FOR THE LEARNING COMMUNITY

In the following chapters we will examine various tools and practices that will enable us to become strong leaders as we develop learning communities. Some tools will assist us in a specific discipline, while others will address multiple disciplines. In addition to assisting us in the disciplines, the tools and practices will help provide answers to three questions:

1. Who and where are we now? Or to put it another way, what is the current reality of our congregational life?

2. Where do we feel that God is calling us to go?

3. How are we going to get there? This question addresses the specific means and actions necessary for a congregation to become what God is calling it to be.

Together these questions, along with the Holy Spirit, can provide the catalyst to motivate a congregation toward learning as a community.

Initially, we will more fully consider *systems thinking*, a prerequisite to all the other tools and the essence of oversight. Other tools and perspectives will include *appreciative inquiry*—a method of intervention that identifies and uses the healthiest aspects of a congregational system; it thereby initiates a self-reinforcing momentum that begins to move the congregation forward as values are identified and a shared vision is developed. Appreciative inquiry helps foster a dialogue between individual visions that emerge through the discipline of personal mastery and a shared vision for the entire congregation. *Congregational culture analysis* will help us to see the deep-seated mental models and assumptions that unconsciously influence the behavior of a congregation.

Scenario planning is a way of mapping out a future for a congregation in ever-changing, uncertain times. It is a process for developing a variety of potential scenarios from which appropriate contingency plans can be strategically developed. Scenario planning is another tool for unearthing and addressing mental models.

Looking at the whole requires discipline and practice, but there are tools to help us with the task. Systems thinking, appreciative inquiry, congregational culture analysis, and scenario planning are four tools that will enable leaders to develop congregations as learning communities able to respond faithfully to God's call and the mission of the church in the 21st century.

Tools for Systems Thinking

The temptation in applying systems theory to congregations is simply to create a systems-analysis model that allows us to get everything happening in the congregational system on one page so that we can examine it piece by piece. Peter Senge recognizes the usefulness of these models in diagramming, analyzing, and redesigning organizational processes, but he also addresses their fallacy. He argues that they produce a "static snapshot of how a system works at a moment in time."[14] The implication of such a tool is to rearrange the components of the system to achieve a more ideal picture. For instance, by using such a model to analyze the programs and ministries of a congregation, we might observe many Christian education offerings for small children but none for youth and adults. Consequently, we would balance out these educational programs by offering more for youth and adults.

We also notice that although a pastoral-care team is in place, none of our shut-in parishioners is being visited. The pastor sends a memo to the chair of the pastoral-care team, reminding him to start having the team visit the shut-ins. As we identified other incongruent elements in the snapshot, we would adjust them appropriately. Senge correctly points out that these types of systems-analysis tools "offer no understanding of how problems we have today have developed over time, . . . nor will they help in understanding the likely consequences of our future efforts at change, especially where we might we might take actions that might make things better today but worse tomorrow."[15] For example, we would have fixed the problems of having no educational offerings for youth and adults, and no visits to shut-ins; but we would not know what created these situations or what actions we should take to prevent such lapses in the future.

Although none of these models or tools that I have seen does harm (in fact many can be helpful in terms of assessment), none of them can get at the deep dynamic structure that we need to identify if we are to understand a congregation systemically. If we believe that congregations are innately dynamic, complex systems, why would we ever think it possible to get a realistic, systemic depiction of them on one page that would remain valid for more than a few seconds?

There is a wonderful story about six blind monks who encounter an elephant. Each monk reaches out and touches a different part of the animal and arrives at a different interpretation of this object they have come upon. One falls against the elephant's broad side and thinks it is a wall. The second feels its tusk and believes it is a spear. The third grabs its trunk and thinks it is like a snake. The fourth feels its knee and decides it is a tree. The fifth touches its ear and says it is like a fan. The final one grabs its tail and declares that it is like a rope.

The story illustrates how we so often behave in congregations. Our focus is on the specific to the exclusion of the whole. To admonish someone to "look at the whole, think systemically!" sounds easy enough, but anyone who has tried this exercise beyond the simplest of situations knows what a difficult challenge it is. Part of the difficulty is that systems thinking seems to be an unnatural act, at least for most of us enculturated in Western society. We have been raised in a context that values and affirms linear thinking and rational thought. We think A + B = C. We speak *subject-verb-object*. The good news is that although it seems unnatural, the practice of systems thinking is very natural. Children can learn systems thinking more easily than adults, because they have not yet been as thoroughly enculturated as the rest of us in the linear process.

Our inclination is to focus our energy so exclusively on what happened that sometimes we forget to ask *why* it happened. We become consumed with events and fail to discern recurring patterns and trends and, at a deeper level, the structures that encourage the repeated patterns.

In systems thinking we think and see in circles instead of lines. For instance, instead of seeing a situation in which A affects B, causing C, we might consider that, yes, A affects B, but C also affects A. Now, at best this sequence is mildly confusing, if not irritating. Possibly a more specific example will demonstrate two important systems-thinking tools, behavior-over-time graphs and causal-loop diagrams.

Trinity Church, Centreville, has experienced rapid numerical growth in the last three years. If we were to drop in at the neighborhood coffee shop and query the local constituency about what caused this development, the answers would probably be simple and linear. "It's that new young pastor, Reverend Owensby. You know, he plays the guitar and does wonderful children's sermons." Or, "Well, of course you realize that at Trinity they are preserving the biblical understanding of Christianity and not buying into all this liberal hogwash that has caused the decline of the last 20 years."

Now, the truth is that Pastor Owensby's children's sermons have probably contributed to the recent membership growth, but the sermons and even Pastor Owensby himself play only small roles in this systemic phenomenon of growth. To see and to understand what is happening in this congregation, we require a view that goes beyond a single and isolated perspective.

Let's examine the activities at Trinity, Centreville, from a more systemic, behavior-over-time perspective. The worship attendance at Trinity from 1974 to 1994 averaged 52. If we graphed the attendance for that period, it would look like a series of mountain peaks:

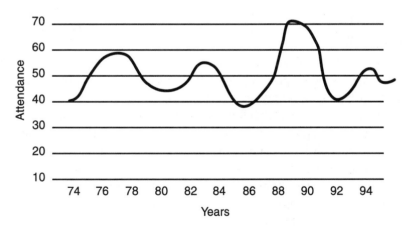

Behavior over Time (BOT)

From this graph we can see a recurring pattern. Attendance goes up, plateaus for a while, and then slowly declines. If we had talked to people before formulating this graph, we would have heard various explanations for past attendance fluctuations. Growth or decline was attributed to—or blamed on—particular clergy, contextual issues, or events in the congregation or the local community. These factors can certainly influence growth; however, sometimes when we examine these factors and explanations alongside the behavior-over-time graph, other influences and causes emerge.

Before Pastor Owensby's arrival, the church had been averaging 53 people at the main 11:00 A.M. Sunday service. When Pastor Owensby first explored the possibility of coming to Trinity Church, he called an old college friend who lived in Centreville. Bill told Pastor Owensby that his wife, Carol, had been shopping for a church for them and their four children (ages two to 13) to attend, but someone had told her that Trinity was not child-friendly; there was no nursery, no Sunday school, and no youth group.

After Pastor Owensby accepted the call to Trinity Church, he contacted Bill and told him that if he would give Trinity another shot, Owensby would work to make the place child-friendly. There were only two rooms off the vestibule that could possibly be used as a nursery. One was the memorial parlor, full of expensive antiques and oriental rugs, and the other was the pastor's office. Although the parlor was never used, except as a dressing room for the bride before a wedding, Pastor Owensby knew that his office was the only politically feasible location for the Sunday nursery. He asked his wife, Alice, to staff the nursery for the first three months, with the agreement that she was making a onetime commitment and would never staff it again.

On Pastor Owensby's first Sunday, Bill and Carol came and even brought their new neighbors. Several lapsed members and other curious residents of the community showed up to check out the new parson.

Pastor Owensby preached a well-crafted sermon about the church's responsibility to equip families for spiritual formation. At the offertory he had the smaller children come forward; taught them a chorus, accompanying himself on the guitar; and gave a children's sermon. Within that service a burst of enthusiasm sprang forth. With 72 in attendance, the church felt fuller than it had in a long time.

But even more important from a systemic perspective is that after the burst of enthusiasm at that first service, word traveled around town that the new people who attended the opening service were pleased with what they had experienced. These newcomers went to work the next day, told others about their experience, and the next Sunday brought their friends with them to church. Their friends told more people, and within a short time people around town began to talk about what was going on over at Trinity.

What began to happen at Trinity was not as simple as a new pastor coming to town and giving good children's sermons. Pastor Owensby strategically built on his arrival by reaching out to a specific group in the community that was being ignored, thereby creating the initial momentum. But the exponential growth began as people experienced a positive worship experience and told others, who in turn had positive experiences and told still others. The dynamics of Trinity's growth can best be described in a circle called a causal-loop diagram.

The positive worship experience causes people to talk and invite friends.

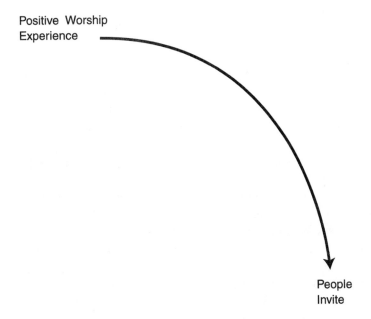

Positive Worship
Experience

People
Invite

As people invite their friends, the attendance rises, and that increase enhances the worship experience.

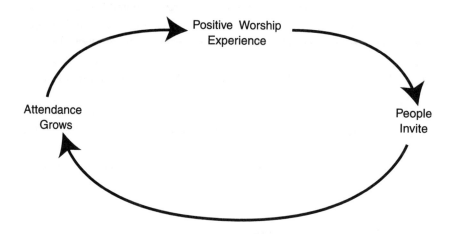

This causal-loop diagram illustrates what in systems thinking is called a "reinforcing feedback loop" and provides a different and more systemic depiction of the growth process. Feedback loops are the basic building blocks of systems thinking, and reinforcing feedback loops illustrate a dynamic phenomenon seen in many settings and situations. Such descriptive expressions as "We're on a roll now!" or "The situation is snowballing!" indicate that a system is experiencing reinforcing feedback. Reinforcing feedback can also go in the opposite direction, creating what we sometimes refer to as a vicious cycle or a downward spiral. A feedback loop is equally helpful in understanding and explaining a decline in church attendance.

Of course, self-reinforcing growth does not continue forever, and an outside force can intervene in the form of "balancing feedback," another building block in systems thinking. "Balancing processes seek equilibrium: They try to bring things to a desired state and keep them there. They also limit and constrain change generated by reinforcing feedback."[16]

A thermostat regulating the temperature in your home is a good example of balancing feedback. The purpose of a thermostat is to maintain a specific temperature. If the temperature outside dropped to zero, the temperature in your home would begin to drop as well until it reached the temperature set on the thermostat. Then the heat would come on and bring the temperature back up to the proper level. Implicit to balancing feedback is a goal. It is the gap between the goal, or the desired level, and the actual level that initiates the feedback. Balancing feedback stabilizes a system.

The "Behavior-over-Time" graph of Trinity Church's attendance during the lengthy period preceding Pastor Owensby's tenure looks like a series of mountain peaks. Attendance would build up to about 70, hold that level for several months, and then coast back down to about 45. The balancing feedback in this situation was the limited seating capacity of the small worship space. Trinity would naturally grow until the seating became limited, and then it would lose momentum and begin a decline.

During the two years of growth following the arrival of Pastor Owensby, a Sunday school was started, as well as a men's group. Then right when attendance was about to break 100, the growth pattern plateaued, and nothing that the congregation could do seemed to matter. The plateau was especially frustrating for those who realized that Centreville was growing at the phenomenal rate of 20 percent a year. Systemically the plateau looked like this:

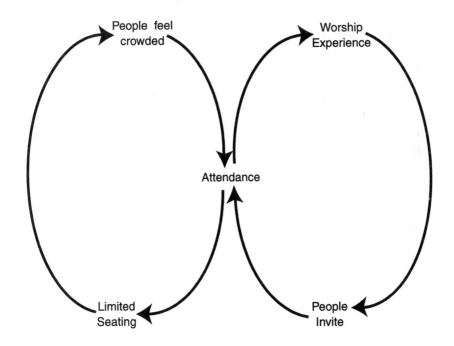

Finally, Pastor Owensby remembered something he had read—that churches plateau after reaching 80 percent of their seating capacity. He decided to launch another worship service at 9:00 A.M. Because the 11:00 service had grown, the church had experienced some conflict over the influx of families and children. Someone had said, "It's like we're being invaded and taken over." Others had complained to the bishop about the children's sermon, saying it was not liturgically correct. Pastor Owensby decided that maybe the 9:00 service could cater to the young families, thus taking the stress off the more traditional crowd at 11:00 A.M. He organized a core group of young families and even got an article published in the local paper about the new service designed for families with children.

When the second service was added, it successfully circumvented the stabilizing force of the balancing feedback process (with one service the pews had been 80 percent full), and the reinforcing cycle of growth began again.

However, there can be other balancing feedback forces besides limited seating. Centreville is a small, rural community, and Trinity Church is a pastoral-size church (50 to 150 members) with all the dynamics that go with being a pastoral church.[17] Members expect the priest to be at the heart of all the activities and ministry of the parish. He is the center and lifeblood of programs, education, pastoral care, evangelism, and administration, and has even been known to rake the leaves when the sexton did not get around to it. Add to that the expectation that Pastor Owensby make home visits to each family on a regular basis, not just in a time of crisis. And the truth is, Pastor Owensby loves to make those visits. His personality is extroverted and gregarious, and his image of the ordained ministry is very similar to the village pastor of the 19th century.

Pastor Owensby lives to be with people, but with the expanding membership, it is becoming more and more difficult for him to spread himself across the varied responsibilities. Consequently, he has little time or energy for thinking or planning strategically. It is as if he were running frantically from one fire to the next. He knows that the congregation is nearing capacity again (together both services now average a total of 171), but he simply lacks the energy even to suggest a third service. A plateau seems inevitable. And what is worse, people are beginning to complain that he is not as available as their former priest, who spent much time not only visiting in homes but also getting to know members of the community at the coffee shop. If we were to depict these additional dynamics in the form of a balancing feedback loop in relation to the reinforcing feedback loop, it might look like this:

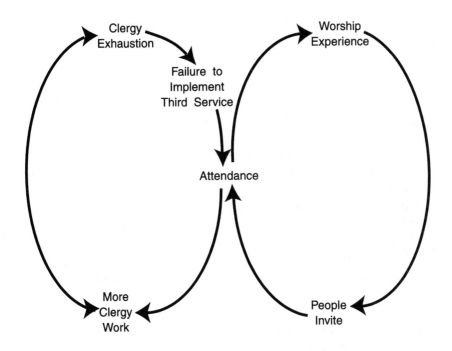

The combination of this reinforcing feedback loop with the balancing feedback loop creates a systems archetype—a pattern of systemic structure that recurs again and again in different settings. Archetypes are classic stories of structural behavior that are seen repeatedly. The one illustrated above is called "the limits to growth" and was first recognized by systems theorist Donella Meadows.

Another building block in systems thinking is the concept of delay. Virginia Anderson and Lauren Johnson, authors and consultants in systems thinking, describe delays this way:

In many systemic structures, delays play a hidden but important role. Delays themselves are neither good nor bad; it's how we humans handle them that determines whether they'll cause trouble.[18]

In our present day, when we expect instant results and events happening with the efficiency and immediacy of a fast-food restaurant, we are susceptible more than ever before to delays affecting our perception and decision-making.

Let's imagine that in response to the demanding pastoral load, rather than hiring an assistant, Pastor Owensby creates a lay pastoral-care team. He persuades the congregation to commit a considerable amount of time and money to pay for his being trained to train others. Twelve people are recruited, trained, and commissioned in a Sunday service as lay pastoral caregivers. The team starts with a great deal of enthusiasm, each member eager to serve in the ministry.

Unfortunately, few people call on their services. Most people request a visit from Pastor Owensby, even in situations that are not critical. The pastor is frustrated because after all the time and money, and his willingness to meet one evening a week for support and further training, no one seems willing to make use of this ministry, and he is still expected to respond personally to every case.

Often we implement well-thought-out strategies that are received well initially, only to experience an absence of positive results. In Pastor Owensby's case, we see a classic systemic delay: The congregation needs a lot more time, teaching, and experimentation before it is willing to change how the pastoral care of the congregation is handled. Pastor Owensby's temptation, as well as that of the pastoral care team, is to give up the idea before it has had a chance to take hold. Pastor Owensby's strategic task at this point is to develop some ways to shorten the delay.

We could easily continue to diagram the development of Trinity Church, but we would never get the entire, complex congregational system on one page. However, we could identify some of the higher leverage points in the system that are necessary to make positive and productive change.

Probably the simplest systems-thinking tool is called "The Five Whys." It should be familiar to any parent of a typically inquisitive six-year-old. When faced with an issue that you suspect is systemic, just ask why. In response to the answer, ask why again and again, and so forth. Sometimes we can get beneath the layers of events to patterns and eventually to structures just by persistently asking why.

For instance, you might wonder why there always seems to be excessive confusion in the acolyte vesting area before worship. At first you think it is because the acolytes that day are rowdy and disrespectful. Then you realize that the situation persists, no matter which children serve as acolytes. Now you are beginning to wonder if it is the acolyte master's fault. Obviously, he lacks the skills necessary to control children. You ask the kids to hold it down every Sunday and give your lecture about preparing themselves for worship, but nothing seems to help. Maybe if you stopped lecturing and pointing your finger long enough to step back from the event, you could see a pattern. Let's say you met with the acolytes and asked them, "Hey guys, tell me, why are things so chaotic in the vesting room right before worship?" One child says, "Well, Pastor, I'm always real excited because I love serving as an acolyte, and I have a hard time concentrating and settling down." You say, "I can understand that because I'm excited too, but besides being excited, why do you think you have a hard time concentrating and settling down?" The child says, "It is always so busy in here with people coming and going."

At that point you realize that the acolytes are so rowdy because the vesting room is between the vestibule and the nursery, and an intermittent stream of parents and small children moves through the vesting area. The rooms are basically the same size, so you propose to the administrative board that the rooms be swapped so that parents can drop children off directly from the vestibule and the acolytes will have the back room to themselves.

Systems thinking is an ongoing discipline that requires practice, and these are just a few of the tools that can be helpful in our effort to discover the underlying structures that influence the behavior of a congregation.

CHAPTER 3

Appreciative Inquiry

Often when a congregation considers its life together, the discussion focuses on what is wrong or what does not work or what the congregation lacks. As a consultant, I am seen by some people as one who has come to fix the problem. And consultants tend to see themselves in this role, either as experts with the information or knowledge to fix the problem, or as process facilitators who enable a congregation to correct how they go about doing things. Appreciative inquiry is a simple method that approaches the congregation from a much different perspective. Instead of focusing on the problem or the incongruencies of a congregation, appreciative inquiry identifies the places in the congregation that are the healthiest and most life giving.

David Cooperrider, professor of organizational behavior science at Case Western Reserve University in Cleveland, developed appreciative inquiry, and a wide variety of organizations use the process. Through structured interviews the process identifies the healthiest, most life-producing aspects of a congregation and then builds upon those strengths to create a new future. Cooperrider says that appreciative inquiry poses questions that ask us to attend to the best of the past and present to ignite the collective imagination of what might be. The aim is to generate new knowledge that expands the "realm of the possible" and helps members of an organization envision a collectively desired future. It enables them to carry forth that vision in ways that successfully translate images of possibility or intentions into reality, and belief into practice.[19]

INTERVENING AT THE HEALTHY PLACES

Appreciative inquiry invites people, instead of wallowing in the quagmire of problems, to imagine what might be. Rather than focusing on what they do not like, appreciative inquiry asks people what they value about their congregation when it is at its best.

> Appreciative Inquiry is an approach to organizational analysis and learning that is uniquely intended for discovering, understanding, and fostering innovations in social organizational arrangements and processes. Appreciative Inquiry refers to both a search for knowledge and a theory of intentional collective action which are designed to evolve the vision and will of a group organization, or society as a whole. It is an inquiry process that affirms our symbolic capacities of imagination and mind as well as our social capacity for conscious choice and cultural evolution. The art of appreciation is the art of discovering and valuing those factors that give life to an organization or group. The process involves interviewing and storytelling to draw the best of the past to set the stage for effective visualization of what might be.[20]

Appreciative inquiry's emphasis on inquiry as a process is rooted in the proposition that one intervenes and initiates some level of change simply by asking questions. How you ask questions, and the questions asked, will determine the focus of the intervention and to that degree influence the outcome. For example, a judicatory representative may pay a visit to a congregation and at a meeting with the administrative board begin by asking, "Well, are you having any sorts of problems I should know about?" This one question has established an agenda, regardless of what items may be listed on the official agenda already handed out. The administrative board's response is to focus in on the most problematic part of the congregation with the assumption that if these parts are corrected, the congregation will become healthier. It sounds reasonable, but this theory is based on a view of the congregational system as a machine; if we can just get the various parts tuned and tweaked, it will run like a sewing machine.

By intervening at the healthiest parts of a congregation, we begin on a foundation that is life giving and fertile with an entirely different vista of possibilities. This generative, creative positioning at the start explains why appreciative inquiry is a vital tool for organizational learning.

Appreciative inquiry operates from four critical perspectives. The first is that the inquiry is appreciative; it assumes that no matter how sick a congregation may be, somewhere in this organic community of people is a place of life and health that enables the system to work to some degree. First and foremost, the inquiry should discover this healthy place and value it.

Second, the inquiry should lead to information and knowledge that is applicable. In other words, we are not going to poke around the insides of a congregation for the thrill of it. The outcome should be useful. If there has been a weakness in the congregational-studies movement, it is that too often congregations have been entered, questioned, surveyed, and basically opened up on the operating table with little useful outcome.

Third, the inquiry should be provocative; appreciative knowledge of "what is" becomes provocative to the extent that what is learned through the inquiry takes on a normative value for members. In a Christian context, the learning and knowledge provoked by the appreciative process fosters a posture in which the community is open to the working of the Holy Spirit and what God is calling it to do.

Fourth, the inquiry is collaborative. "This principle assumes an inseparable relationship between the process of inquiry and its content."[21] A mechanic can objectively tinker with my car, because it is a machine and he is not a part of the machine; but when we intervene in an organic congregational system, we and our process influence the congregation systemically, and at one level we become participants in the system. We are not the separate, totally objective observers that we tend to think we are.

Appreciative inquiry recognizes three types of reality that affect a congregation: historical, current, and anticipatory. Historical reality includes those experiences from our past that still affect who we are and how we behave, such as a congregation's involvement with the civil rights movement, or a time when the congregation experienced a great religious revival. Such events still have an effect on the congregation's identity and consequently on how it behaves. As I explained earlier, current reality is where the congregation is now, at this moment.

Anticipatory reality is the reality we can imagine or envision for the future. It creates a catalytic image that draws us forward into what God is calling us to be and do. Anticipatory reality is the source of a vision's power. Appreciative inquiry identifies the healthiest, most life-giving parts of a congregational system and uses them as a foundation to create an anticipatory reality and to build a shared vision of the future.

Another aspect of appreciative inquiry is the understanding that organizations and individuals are heliotropic. That is, just as a plant in the window is drawn toward the sunlight, we are drawn toward those images that give us life. If we are able to discover and raise up those healthy aspects of a congregation, then we can create life-giving images that will attract the entire system. One of the most convincing examples of this understanding is the now famous Pygmalion experiment:

> In the classic Pygmalion study, teachers are led to believe on the basis of "credible" information that some of their students possess exceptionally high potential while others do not. In other words, the teachers are led, on the basis of some expert opinion, to hold a positive image (PT) or expectancy of some students and a negative image (NT) or expectancy of others. Unknown to the teachers however, is the fact that the so-called high-potential groupings were selected at random; in objective terms, all student groupings were equivalent in potential and are merely dubbed as high, regular, or low potential. Then, as the experiment unfolds, differences quickly emerge, not on the basis of any innate intelligence factor or some other predisposition but solely on the basis of the manipulated expectancy of the teacher. Over time, subtle changes among students evolve into clear differences as the high PT students begin to significantly overshadow all others in actual achievement.[22]

What is true for individuals is true for those organisms made up of individuals which we call congregations. Four basic steps are involved in the appreciative inquiry process.

1. DISCOVER AND VALUE THE BEST OF "WHAT IS"

As has been described, at this entry step the task is to find the healthiest, most life-giving parts of the congregation, the stories of times past or present that regenerate a sense of calling and passion. As these narratives emerge, it is important to determine the factors and forces that made them possible. Retelling these stories is an affirming experience that enables participants to identify what they truly value about the congregation.

2. DREAM AND ENVISION "WHAT MIGHT BE"

Within the creative context of valuing and celebrating the best of what is, envisioning is a natural development. An environment is created where people are willing to risk imagining what God might do in their lives, because what God has done before is once again alive and real, remembered in the biblical sense. One reason we continually immerse ourselves in retelling the biblical story is that as the story of what God has done for God's people comes vividly to life again, we can imagine and believe what God is capable of doing for us. Similarly, this dynamic of remembering is true also for more recent stories of what God has done for us in our lives through the ministry of a specific congregation.

3. DESIGN: DIALOGUING "WHAT SHOULD BE"

Noted quantum physicist David Bohm identifies the ability to suspend judgment as one of the prerequisites for true dialogue, which to Bohm is a level of communication entirely different from and superior to regular discussion. In normal discussion we tend to bounce our opinions and positions back and forth. Bohm reminds us that the root word for discussion is the same as that for percussion.[23] I present my view, and you present yours. Often in discussion our objective is to persuade the other person to listen to and agree with us. Sometimes when I am discussing something that I really care about, I am formulating my next response to what is being said without really listening to the speaker. True dialogue involves a level of communication at which we suspend our opinions and preconceived notions in an atmosphere of collegial trust. Dialogue helps to challenge and focus our visions and engages people's ownership and commitment. The affirming, trust-building nature of appreciative inquiry creates the climate for the necessary step of dialogue to occur.

4. Co-construct the Future

At this stage we approach the organizational structure of the congregation as if we were architectural engineers with an eye to what changes need to be made to move the congregation toward the shared vision. How might our style of leadership need to change? What resources, human and financial, will we need for this journey? Should we reconfigure how we work together as an administrative board? Maybe we should organize around specific strategic tasks in teams? What are the three objectives we need to accomplish in the next six months to move toward our vision? What strategic tasks does each of us feel a passion about individually?

At this point some basic action planning can be helpful, but it is good to keep in mind that sometimes we restrict creative learning in congregations by overstructuring and controlling. Congregational transformations seem to take on a self-sustaining, self-organizing life of their own because of the self-reinforcing feedback that I described in chapter 2. Sometimes it is better to sit back and watch the organizational structures begin to emerge rather than overmanaging the situation and interfering with the transformation's natural development.

> Appreciative inquiry establishes a momentum of its own. Members of the organization find innovative ways to help move the organization closer to the ideal. Because the ideals are grounded in realities, there is the confidence to try to make things happen. This is important to underscore because it is precisely because of the visionary content, placed in juxtaposition to grounded examples of the extraordinary, that appreciative inquiry opens the status quo to transformations in collective action.[24]

The Interview Process

The interview used in the first step begins in a generic format nonspecific as to topic. The generic interview is broad and general; it is used with a core group of leaders from the congregation. With the data recorded from this initial interview, the leaders customize the interview into a form most appropriate to the congregational setting and the areas that the congregation wants to address. I think it is helpful to insert the name of the congregation in the interview. Here is an example of questions for an initial interview.

1. Looking at your entire experience at Grace Church, remember a time when you felt most alive, most fulfilled, or most excited about your involvement in the church.
   (a) What made it exciting?
   (b) Who else was involved?
   (c) Describe how you felt about it.
2. Without being humble, what do you value most about yourself as a person and as a member of Grace Church?
3. What do you value most about Grace Church?
4. What is the most important thing your church has contributed to your life?
5. What is the core ingredient in Grace Church's makeup, without which Grace Church would just not be Grace Church?
6. Make three wishes for the future of Grace Church.

Even in the most depressed congregations, embers of life still glow that can be fanned into a blazing spiritual fire. Our challenge is to locate these embers of spiritual health and life. Appreciative inquiry provides a process for unearthing and putting to use these life-giving aspects of a congregation to initiate new life and a shared vision.

If we were to use these generic questions with a core group of people in a congregation, we might hear a story like this one:

1. Looking at your entire experience at Grace Church, remember a time when you felt most alive, most fulfilled, or most excited about your involvement in the church.
   (a) What made it exciting?
   (b) Who else was involved?
   (c) Describe how you felt about it.

About three years after Mary and I joined Grace Church, there was a family in town whose house burned down. They weren't members of the church, but a group of us got together and helped them get into some temporary housing. Later, with some help from area merchants, we spearheaded a drive to help them rebuild their home. Every Sunday we prayed for this family and for our effort. Over a hundred volunteers participated in the project, and when we finished there was this

*great celebration and housewarming. Pastor Harris asked me
to present the family with a bottle of wine and a loaf of bread
on behalf of the church. As I gave them the bread, I said something I remembered from the old Jimmy Stewart movie* It's a
Wonderful Life, *about wine being for joy and bread for new
life. And when I looked into those people's faces and the faces
of all who had gathered there, I realized that I had never done
anything like this building project in my life, and for the first
time I felt like I was a part of the church—not just coming on
Sundays and doing church, but all of us were gathered there
actually being the church, being the body of Christ in the
world.*

Stories like this one enable people to return to that place deep in their
hearts where values reside and visions are born. This place in the heart is
often dormant, and we rarely have time to visit, but when we do, something
happens, and the Holy Spirit initiates a momentum that inspires and engages
us all. We call this first question in the interview the "fateful question,"
because it sets the climate in which these following questions are answered.

2.   Without being humble, what do you value most about yourself as a
     person and as a member of Grace Church?

     *That's really a difficult question to answer, but I guess it is
     that I am willing to help people however I can.*

3.   What do you value most about Grace Church?

     *What I value most is that once we get clear on what we want to
     do, everyone pulls together and sees it through to the end. I
     think we make a difference here in our city.*

4.   What is the most important thing your church has contributed to your
     life?

     *The most important thing is that it is a place where I feel con-
     nected to people. We've been through a lot together, and I can
     trust these people. Most of my family lives out on the West
     Coast, so Grace Church is kind of like my family here.*

5. What is the core ingredient in Grace Church's makeup, without which Grace Church would just not be Grace Church?

Grace Church would not be Grace Church if we didn't care about those beyond our four walls, people in the community who are in need. We've always been the church in town that steps up to the plate when catastrophe strikes.

6. Make three wishes for the future of Grace Church.

I hope that we can do more in the community, especially working together with other churches or agencies like Habitat for Humanity. I would also like to see us grow with some younger families and children. None of us are getting any younger. Finally, I'd like to see us reaching out to the community's young people, not just our kids but all the community.

After gathering interview data from the core leadership, we would look for common themes or issues. If there was a consensus on something like the church's commitment to outreach ministry in the community, we could customize the interview process to focus on this area. The core leadership would then proceed to interview the rest of the congregation. The customized interview would look like this:

1. Looking at your entire involvement with Grace Church's outreach ministry to the community, remember a time when you felt most alive, most fulfilled, or most excited about your involvement.
   (a) What made it exciting?
   (b) Who else was involved?
   (c) Describe how you felt about it.
2. Without being humble, what do you value most about your contribution to the outreach ministry?
3. What do you value most about the outreach ministry?
4. What has been the greatest benefit of your involvement in the outreach ministry?
5. What is the core ingredient in Grace Church's outreach ministry without which the ministry would not have been meaningful and effective?
6. What opportunities do you see in the community for further ministry by Grace Church?

7. Make three wishes for the future of Grace Church's outreach ministry to the community.

If there were no predominant themes or issues, you would simply use the same interview that you used with the core leadership.

Many times strategic efforts to re-engineer, restructure, redevelop, transform, and re-envision fail because they basically involve wiping the slate clean and dreaming up the ideal structures and programs for a new day in a congregation or judicatory. These efforts fail because they are not rooted in the actual culture, values, and identity of the people who make up these institutions. The new ideas and programs that we generate may be excellent, but if they are not consistent with who we are as Christians and who we are as a congregation, they rarely achieve the desired results.

Another way of saying it is that new behaviors and practices must be connected to the deepest parts of a congregation's heart. Appreciative inquiry opens up that heart and allows those parts to be elements in the process of formulating the new behaviors and practices. Being rooted in the deepest levels of the congregational culture happens naturally as a part of the process.

CHAPTER 4

Congregational Culture Analysis

One of the challenges of entering a new congregation is trying to decipher the mystery of why things happen the way they do. One tool that
helps me understand a congregation is a process I call "congregational culture analysis." By culture I do not mean the external culture but rather the
internal culture of the congregation. Congregational culture is invisible at its
deepest level. It includes those norms, rules, understandings, symbols, and
metaphors that one doesn't learn about on the first visit. In fact, congregational culture is the stuff that no one communicates to a newcomer formally, at least not for a long time. The deepest level of congregational culture is "the way we do things around here," ways that are never formally
articulated.

For example, at the early service we don't unlock the front door, because everyone just knows that we use the side door for the early service.
This understanding is a shared assumption in the congregation. If you are
patient enough and wait around, you will discover a stream of people coming out the side door. Eventually, after several years you become fully
enculturated, aware of the tacit knowledge. In fact, the culture begins to
shape the way you look at things.

John Kotter, professor of leadership at Harvard Business School, asserts that one reason efforts at organizational transformation fail is that
new practices and new behaviors do not get rooted deeply in the culture;

eventually the old behaviors reemerge, and the new behaviors and practices get pushed aside and disappear.[25] We need to come to an understanding of our congregational culture because it can help explain some of the incomprehensible, irrational aspects of the congregation; it will help clear up some of the mysteries. We need to understand culture because these shared assumptions can be a source of resistance to a congregational transformation. A culture is established in a congregation by the first formal and informal leaders, and it is changed by subsequent leadership. Internal culture cannot be changed until a leader identifies and names it.

We also need to understand congregational culture because if leaders do not become conscious of the internal culture, then it is possible that the culture will shape them to fit. The culture of a congregation subtly affects the behavior of leaders, and over time it will change the leaders to better fit the culture. If the congregation is healthy, this change is a positive benefit, but if the congregation is unhealthy, leaders will take on unhealthy characteristics as they become more a part of the congregation. It is critical that leaders understand the way congregations function, the procedure by which decisions are made, and the real structures of power and authority—and that these elements are almost always invisible initially. Examining the internal culture is one way to discover these aspects of a congregation.

Edgar Schein, of MIT's Sloan School of Management, says that this internal culture has three levels, with the highest being the most visible. The highest level consists of artifacts; the second, deeper down, is espoused values; and finally, the nearly invisible basic shared assumptions are the essence of the congregation's culture.[26]

Artifacts

Artifacts are visible and prominent objects, structures, and processes. Artifacts are what I would see and experience if I walked into a place cold—the shape of the building, the vestments, the way insiders go about doing things. They help me answer questions: What's going on here? What do I observe? Artifacts are easy to identify but hard to decipher and understand. Once when I visited a conference center for the first time, I noticed that many of the doors were left unlocked—ones that I would have expected to find bolted shut. When I arrived at the conference center, I was the only one on campus except for the staff. The director took me into the kitchen and said, "If you're hungry, here's food. Just come help yourself." I said to myself, "This is an artifact; it means something. The unlocked doors say something about the internal culture of this institution."

Another example of artifacts: A new pastor walks into the church, enters the basement, and finds the nursery located in a damp part of the building, with paint peeling and some old furniture stacked in the corner. Another example: the way people dress, whether it's a $700 suit or jeans and a T-shirt. The general condition of the building and grounds is another example.

For a non-Episcopalian, the first few visits to a typical Episcopal parish are full of identifiable artifacts: using a prayer book, kneeling at certain times in the service, making the sign of the cross, bowing or genuflecting, standing for the reading of the Gospel, reverencing the processional cross. And there are the distinctive vestments, the procession itself, the water in the font, the centrality of the altar, bells ringing at specified times in the liturgy, how clergy are addressed, and the use of terms such as vicar, rector, narthex, nave, the Sanctus, sequence, the Gloria, gradual, sacristy, and vestry.

If you were a non-Christian attending church for the first time and saw the typical offertory during which the ushers gather money in offering plates and then present the plates at the altar, along with gifts of bread and wine as everyone is standing, you would be experiencing a distinctive artifact of the congregation's internal culture. The artifacts you would see and experience in the offertory would be visible, but their respective meanings difficult to decipher.

Once during a presentation on congregational culture, I asked the participants to brainstorm some examples of artifacts, and a man presented what has become my favorite example. The artifact was a six-inch, sterling-silver drinking straw. On his first Sunday serving as priest in the parish, he noticed the straw set out with the communion vessels on the credence table. Perplexed and curious, he asked the altar guild member on duty the purpose of the straw, and she said she did not know. He told her they would not be needing it. The woman protested immediately and said, "Oh no, we have to have the 'silver straw.'" The priest could have exerted his authority and risked initiating a conflict, but instead he had the patience and took the time to explore what the straw meant. He discovered that years before, one of the matriarchs of the church had broken her jaw, and the straw was the means by which the priest administered the communion wine. The woman had long ago recovered from the injury and had since died, but the straw remained.

The silver drinking straw had become obsolete in terms of its original purpose, but it had remained because it was a symbol of a basic shared assumption that the congregation was willing to reach out and minister to someone who required a different means to receive communion. I like this example, because it also illustrates how artifacts can become separated from their original significance.

ESPOUSED VALUES

The next level in congregational culture is espoused values. Espoused values include the strategies, goals, philosophies, doctrines, and theologies that a community formally says it believes and values. A key word here is "espoused," because although we espouse these values, we do not always practice or live by them. Espoused values that we can identify in most churches would include mission statements, such as, "The mission of the church is to restore all persons to unity with God and one another through Jesus Christ." Or a church welcome sign seen as you enter the city that announces, "We're the friendliest church in town!"

Other examples include the vows we make at baptisms, the creeds, ordination services, vision statements, newcomer brochures, and handouts that describe policy and expectations for weddings, funerals, baptisms, or membership. One of the espoused values of all Episcopal churches is our polity. We espouse that we are congregational expressions of a larger church, connected through the ministry of a bishop charged with our pastoral oversight and assisted in that oversight by an ordained priesthood and diaconate as well as by the laity. Espoused values are expressed in all those formal ways through which we announce, "This is who we are, what we are about, and how we do things."

One of my favorite examples of espoused values is the parish profiles developed for clergy search processes. A few years ago my wife was invited to enter the search process at a church in Hawaii. On the opening page of the parish profile, before the reader saw anything specifically about the congregation, was a large postcard-quality photograph of the beach with swaying palm trees at sunset. The scene was attractive and engaging and, I suppose, at one level related to the identity of the congregation.

Often parish profiles are expressions of espoused values—how we would like to be but not necessarily who we are. We may claim that we are an inclusive, open congregation, eager to grow. That description may not reflect the current reality but rather what we hope to become.

SHARED ASSUMPTIONS

At the deepest level of congregational culture are basic shared assumptions. Schein defines basic assumptions as "unconscious, taken-for-granted beliefs, perceptions, thoughts, and feelings (ultimate source of values and action)." Schein explains further: "Basic assumptions, . . . tend to be those we neither confront nor debate and hence are extremely difficult to change. To learn something new in this realm requires us to resurrect, reexamine, and possibly change"[27]—what Senge would call our mental models. Basic shared assumptions are a specific type of mental model—ones that we have developed through shared experience with others in community as we have lived through challenges and problems. With time, these basic assumptions may become incongruent with our context and current reality, a situation that requires leadership to initiate a shared process through which a congregation can surface, challenge, and change the mental models.

Basic shared assumptions derive their power from the fact that after they have become ingrained in the consciousness of a congregation, they begin to operate outside awareness. They are the unwritten, unseen rules, norms, and mental models of a community.

Shortly after my wife and I arrived in Sewanee, Tennessee, we were talking with a colleague and his wife. We mentioned that we had been invited to a hamburger cookout and that the hosts had said that the dress would be casual. Our friend asked, "Did they mean really casual or Sewanee casual?" He and his wife then went on to explain that shortly after their arrival, they had received a similar invitation, so they arrived at a cookout in jeans and discovered everyone else dressed more formally in dresses and trousers, blazers, button-down shirts and ties. The shared assumption in the community is that casual still means a coat and tie, but no one had thought to communicate that in a formal way. You "just know."

Several examples of basic shared assumptions that we could probably surface in many congregations would include:

We've got to control things [or protect something], or the sky will surely fall (often a basic assumption of administrative boards).

Those people wouldn't feel comfortable here.

If I fall flat on my face in the world and fail miserably, I can always come home here, and I will be accepted, forgiven, and loved.

I know the pastor is doing a great job, but eventually he'll mess up like the last one.

Small congregations aren't really churches (a basic assumption sometimes held by small congregations themselves).

Laypeople cannot be trusted to minister (often held by laypeople).

Worshipping together shapes our community.

You must be the member of a particular family to exercise leadership in this congregation.

Somehow, God will provide what we need in order to do what God is calling us to do.

Every member of this community is of value and has a gift and contribution to make to our ministry.

The presbytery [conference, diocese, bishop] is out to get us.

One way to surface basic assumptions is to consider artifacts in light of espoused values. The dialogue between the two will often allow basic assumptions to emerge into the light. For example, in our newcomer's brochure we say that we are a friendly, welcoming congregation, and yet an artifact that can easily be observed is that only the clergy speak to newcomers at the coffee hour. The shared, unspoken assumption here may be that we will incorporate you into our community when you have proved to us that you are going to stay—or that it is the clergy's responsibility to welcome newcomers. Schein offers that basic assumptions

> often deal with fundamental aspects of life—the nature of time and space; human nature and human activities; the nature of truth and how one discovers it; the correct way for the individual and the group to relate to one another, the relative importance of work, family and self-development; the proper role of men and women; and the nature of the family.
> We do not develop new assumptions about each of these areas in every group or organization that we join. Each member of a new group will bring her or his own cultural learning from prior groups, but as the new group develops its own shared history, it will develop modified or brand-new assumptions in critical areas of its experience. Those new assumptions make up the culture of that particular group.[28]

Congregational culture evolves over time through shared experience and the influx of new members. Sometimes the culture forms the members as they adopt the basic assumptions of the congregation, but the assumptions that a new member, particularly a new leader, brings can affect the congregation's culture as well.

Wise leaders will keep their eyes open when entering a new congregation for its varied levels of internal culture, with the understanding that why something happens a certain way may have nothing to do with the espoused values. It may instead be a response to a basic assumption of which the new leader is not yet aware. One of the ongoing tasks of leadership is to manage the healthy integration of the three levels of culture, to create a healthy and consistent alignment of a congregation's artifacts, espoused values, and basic assumptions.

One way for a new pastor to do this task is gently to raise incongruencies as he or she discovers them. Another more elaborate means might be to bring in an outsider to lead a full process of congregational culture analysis. Here is an example of Schein's process, with steps adapted for congregational use:

1. Obtain Leadership Commitment

Delving into the deepest, most mysterious levels of a congregation's life is both intriguing and dangerous. Surfacing the shared assumptions that have provided a level of security and stability to a congregation is almost always an anxiety-producing affair. It can also be an exercise in both trust development and faith formation. Nevertheless, it should be considered a major intervention. To be successful, it should be initiated by a specific issue or concern that will provide the necessary motivation to complete the process. The consultant should be invited, in writing, by the clergy and the administrative board, and it should be clear to everyone why the process is being undertaken.

Examples of purposes for undertaking the process might include:

- Resolving a history of conflicted relationships between clergy and lay leaders.
- Preparing to launch a major outreach ministry that would involve the congregation more deeply in the life of the local community.
- Beginning a parish self-identity study in preparation for receiving new leadership.
- Addressing the inability of a congregation to grow numerically in a location that is demographically conducive to growth.
- Examining a rapid, yet unexplainable decline in attendance and membership.

Within this step the clergy and primary lay leadership should identify the major "culture carriers" in the congregation so that they can be invited into the process. By culture carriers I mean the people who have been a part of the life of the congregation long enough to have a deep sense of ownership and history. They are the people who know the stories of how the congregation has developed over the years. It is also helpful to include some newer people, who will be the most valuable in identifying artifacts. Beyond these two criteria the participants invited should be people involved and interested in the future of the congregation. An appropriate location should be chosen, one that includes a large meeting room as well as smaller "break-out" rooms for small-group work. The following cultural analysis process can be done in a day, but I prefer an overnight retreat.

2. Conduct the Large Group Meeting

This meeting should begin with the clergy or the primary lay leader stating the purpose for implementing the process: "We're entering into this process because we want to discover why, with all of our hard efforts, we can't seem to get off the ground and attract and keep new members. The demographics of our area are exploding, and we have people come for a while, but they don't stay." The consultant is then introduced; he or she proceeds with the following substeps:

(a) Make the presentation. The consultant gives a presentation on congregational culture that defines and differentiates the three levels. As the presentation proceeds, it is helpful to invite participants to try to think of a few examples of each of the three levels.

(b) Identify artifacts. At this step, the group brainstorms a list of the congregation's artifacts. Sometimes it is helpful to include some of the newest members of the congregation in this exercise. The consultant can also be helpful in identifying artifacts.

(c) Identify espoused values. What do we say we believe? Once this list is fully developed, the group is invited to consider the espoused values in light of the artifacts. Which values seem consistent with the artifacts, which do not, and why? This comparison can lead to lengthy discussion. It is important to maintain a spirit of joint inquiry as you progress, because you want to keep people involved and taking ownership of the process. This discussion will lead into the next step, which deals with basic shared assumptions. If you are having an overnight retreat, this is a good place to stop for the evening.

(d) Make a first cut at basic assumptions. Schein advises that "the key to getting at the underlying assumptions is to check whether the espoused values that have been identified really explain all of the artifacts or whether things that have been described as going on have clearly not been explained or are in actual conflict with some of the values articulated."[29] For example, one of the espoused values might be that "we are a welcoming community that reaches out to families." Yet, in the list of artifacts we see a dreary, ill-equipped nursery with no staff or volunteers. This incongruence may imply a basic assumption

that although we want families with children, parents are expected to take care of their own youngsters with no help from the church. If there is an inconsistency between an artifact and an espoused value, the way to discover the basic shared assumption is to have an honest conversation about why we say one thing but do another.

3. Identify Cultural Aids and Hindrances

For this step, separate the group into smaller working groups of four to six people and assign the following task:

(a) Each group is to spend an hour refining the assumptions and identifying any other basic assumptions that might have been missed in the larger group.

(b) Take 20 to 30 minutes and categorize the assumptions as to whether they will aid or hinder addressing the identified issue.

It is extremely important for the groups to try to maintain a balance in their consideration of hindrances and aids, because our inclination is to overemphasize the hindrances and fail to recognize the usefulness of the cultural aids. Schein argues, "Culture change probably arises more from identifying assumptions that will aid than from changing assumptions that will hinder."[30]

4. Report Assumptions and Joint Analysis

In this step we attempt to reach an agreement as to which basic assumptions are the most important and have the most significance for the congregation's issue or concern. A good question at this point is, "What ramifications do these assumptions have for what we feel God is calling us to do as a congregation?"

Let's imagine that Christ Church in Anytown, USA, has conducted a congregational culture analysis in an effort to decide whether to start a new ministry to young single adults. Demographic information and surveys show a large and growing sector of young single adults in the community and very little ministry designed to reach them. One of the shared assumptions that emerged from the process: "Christ Church is a place where people will care for you as if you were a member of the family." The task for the leaders at Christ Church is to consider how they can better communicate this shared assumption to this population group. How can this shared assumption be used within the current constituency strategically to support a new ministry to young adults? How can we ease the process by which a young single adult moves from being an inquiring visitor to experiencing the people of Christ Church as a family? What organizational structures at Christ Church need to be changed to further encourage this strength?

One benefit of this process is that some of the information gathered may be useful in considering questions and issues of the congregation beyond the original issue. The analysis of a congregation's culture is a critical thinking skill, a discipline that improves with practice. Although some people have an intuitive gift for discerning the culture of a congregation, it is more useful to discover the culture by some process that involves and encourages the ownership of the community. At the least, simply by educating people about congregational culture, we can develop an ongoing conversation that will encourage the leadership continually to surface its assumptions and mental models and learn together as a congregation.

CHAPTER 5

Scenario Planning

In general, it seems that churches resist planning for the future. I cannot help wondering whether some sort of premillennialist vapor goes to people's heads when they are elected to an administrative board and they begin to think, "Why plan for the future if Jesus is going to return next Tuesday?" To make matters worse, now that many congregations and judicatories have finally recognized the need for strategic planning, they are using processes and methods of long-term strategic planning that assume the simple and stable context of the 1950s.

With a world as complex and ever changing as ours, how does a congregation make any responsible and dependable plans for the future? In this chapter we will explore a planning process that is not only well suited for a changing and complex world, but also an excellent means for challenging our mental models and creating opportunities for team learning.

Scenario planning is a process that creates stories that describe different, though clearly plausible, futures. Peter Schwartz—a leading futurist and president of Global Business Network, an international think tank—describes scenarios as

a tool for ordering one's perceptions about alternative future environments in which today's decisions might be played out. In practice, scenarios resemble a set of stories, written or spoken, built around carefully constructed plots. . . . Stories can express multiple perspectives on complex events; scenarios give meaning to these events.[31]

And in his book *The Art of the Long View: Planning the Future in an Uncertain World*, Schwartz explains:

> Scenarios are a tool for helping us to take a long view in a world of great uncertainty. . . . Scenarios are stories about the way the world might turn out tomorrow, stories that can help us recognize and adapt to changing aspects of our present environment.[32]

Scenario planning is better described as a discipline for thinking from different perspectives than as a formal planning methodology. If we are willing to set aside temporarily our notions and mental models of how the world is going to turn out, scenarios give us the opportunity to develop more than one contingency plan. The ultimate purpose of scenario planning is to challenge our thinking about tomorrow in such a way that we make better decisions today.

There are several variations of the process, but I will describe the one developed by Pierre Wack when he served as senior planning officer for the Royal/Shell Oil Group, as refined by Peter Schwartz. In the early 1970s Wack and his colleague Ted Newland were looking for leading indicators and trends in world politics and the global economy that might affect the price of petroleum, which had remained steady for a long time. Wack and Newland observed several factors, noting for example that the United States was beginning to exhaust its oil reserves, that American demand for oil was rising, and that several Middle Eastern countries were emerging as part of a united coalition known as the Organization of Petroleum Exporting Countries. It became clear to Wack and Newland that OPEC could and probably would increase the price of oil, especially in light of member nations' bitterness toward the United States for supporting Israel in the 1967 six-day Arab-Israeli war. Wack was convinced that at some point OPEC would raise prices.

The two men created two scenarios to present to Shell's directors—one describing basically the then-current approach, following the assumption that things would continue as they were and that oil prices would remain steady. The second scenario described a world in which OPEC raised prices, initiating an oil crisis. Shell's directors listened politely, acknowledging that if the second scenario proved true, they would have to change the way they did business. Then they promptly dismissed the notion.

At this critical point Wack realized that to make full use of scenarios, they could not be viewed simply as another forecasting tool—that in fact, they should not be used as a forecasting tool at all. He realized that for scenarios to make a difference and to serve as a useful tool, they "should be more than water on a stone." They had to "change our manager's view of reality."[33]

In Wack's second attempt he did not present simple stories but vivid, detailed accounts that included various ramifications, and he forcefully described the driving forces in the world that would bring the crisis to a head. This time he got their attention; when the oil crisis hit, Shell was the only oil company that was prepared, that had thought through contingency plans, and that was ready to respond quickly. Consequently, Shell rose from being one of the world's weaker oil companies to one of its strongest and most profitable.

Of course, my interest here is not to make the church profitable; however, if the church could have been fully prepared for the resurgence of the baby-boomer generation's interest in the church back in the 1980s (an interest that has since waned), we could have been better prepared to proclaim the Gospel to an entire generation. A similar challenge faces us now with emerging generations.

If we are successfully to surface and examine mental models that might hinder our view of impending trends and developments and even resources with which we could respond strategically, a simple and effective process is needed. What follows is a variation on Schwartz's process for scenario planning, adapted for use with a congregation.

Before beginning the process you will need to gather a group of 12 to 20 people to work as a team to build the scenarios. A wide variety of perspectives is helpful here, and it is imperative that you use people outside as well as within the congregation. Helpful participants from outside the congregation might include:

- A chamber of commerce director who is knowledgeable about the demographics of the region.
- A local history teacher who would have a grasp of how the local community has developed historically.
- A local artist noted for high creative energy.

A diverse team will enable more divergent perspectives to be explored, and consequently the level of corporate learning will increase. At the same time, include enough significant stakeholders, such as matriarchs and patriarchs of the congregation, to maintain a connection to the parish's identity and culture. Select people from all walks of life for the team. All steps of the process can be done in an overnight retreat.

1. Identify Focal Issue or Decision

Your first task is to identify and focus the specific decision that pertains to the future of the congregation. The decision needs to be relevant and critical; something that will affect or be affected by the larger context of the community: "Should we expand the church staff in the coming five years?" "Should we remodel and expand the worship space?" A question with insufficient weight would be something like, "Should we change the altar frontal from purple to Sarum blue during Advent?" The question should address an issue that affects the congregation's corporate life as a whole. Schwartz encourages building from the inside out:

> [B]egin with a specific decision or issue, then build out toward the environment. What will [your] decision makers. . . . be thinking hard about in the near future? What are the decisions that have to be made that will have a long-term influence?[34]

2. Identify Key Factors in the Local Environment

The task here is for the team to identify and name the factors that would normally inform such a decision. "What will decision-makers want to know when making key choices? What will be seen as success or failure? What are the considerations that will shape those outcomes?"[35] The answers to these questions are what leaders need to know to make responsible decisions. How might this decision affect our life as a congregation, or the life of our surrounding neighborhood?

3. Identify Driving Forces

Brainstorm a list of the larger driving forces that will affect the factors influencing this decision. Consider these forces in terms of social, theological, economic, political, and technological impact. If the decision was whether to start a day-care center, a driving force would be the rising number of dual-profession families, or the rising cost of child care, or the emerging liability issues related to caring for children. Or if the decision was whether to relocate the church to the growing sector of the city, a driving force would be the migration of people to that area, or the changing nature of the current neighborhood. Once these are listed, the group should determine which forces are predetermined and inevitable and which forces are unpredictable or uncertain. Some additional research may be necessary at this point.

4. Rank Driving Forces

As a group, rank the driving forces and factors as to importance and uncertainty. Ultimately in this step participants need to identify two or three forces or factors that are both most important and most uncertain. "Scenarios cannot differ over predetermined elements like the inevitable aging of the baby boomers, because predetermined elements are bound to be the same in all scenarios."[36] Growing old is a predetermined element that lacks uncertainly. The aging of America is certainly a driving force, but it would have a similar effect on any scenario. We are looking for driving forces that are both critically important and highly uncertain.

5. Select the Scenario Logics

The preceding exercise of ranking the driving forces according to importance and uncertainty will determine the axes along which you will determine your scenarios. These axes will run the spectrum between the potential extremes of the uncertain driving forces. This is why it is important to determine the forces that are the most uncertain and yet most important to the decision. Let's assume that we are trying to determine what type of worship experience emerging generations will be most attracted to.

One driving force would be people's tendency toward a more privatistic spirituality versus a spirituality rooted in corporate community.

Privatistic  Corporate

Consequently, one scenario would tell the story of a world where people exercise a very private, individualistic form of spirituality, whereas in another scenario developed at the other end of the axis, a world would be described in which people are committed predominantly to a corporate, communal spirituality.

The other driving forces will determine additional axes of influence upon the stories. One way to use the axes to determine various scenarios is to cross them and create quadrants of possibilities. For instance, you might add another axis to the one above, depicting at one end a style of worship that is very entertainment-oriented, such as what we see in the Willow Creek experience. (Willow Creek Church, located in a northwestern suburb of Chicago, is a nondenominational "megachurch" that holds "seeker services" featuring rock music geared to younger tastes, and dramatic performances with high production values, targeted to newcomers with no previous church experience.)

At the other end of the axis would be a move toward contemplative, liturgical worship services, such as those using Taizé—a meditative style of music consisting of easy-to-sing choruses, originated in a French religious community. Each quadrant would provide guiding factors for a different story of what the emerging generations will more likely respond to.

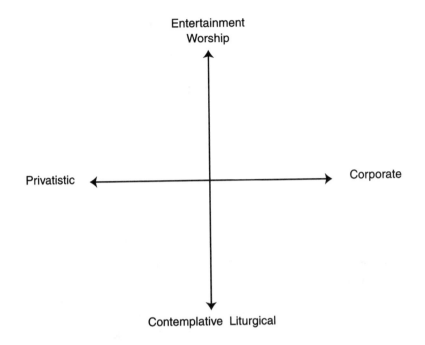

6. FLESH OUT THE SCENARIOS

At this point you will flesh out and develop the narratives; tell the story of how this potential world might look. This activity is best done in smaller groups. If you were using the axes of driving forces related to migration and downtown development, you could divide into four groups. Often it is helpful to allow people some creative fermentation time before they attempt this task. At an overnight retreat, this would be a perfect point to stop for the evening. Or if you are working through the process in one day, you could stop at lunch and allow people some free time before reconvening in mid-afternoon. Sometimes people get their best insights in the shower or even while sleeping. Encourage participants to consider the driving forces and then to turn themselves loose to tell a story imagining the overall context of the decision. Be sure the key factors in step 2 are addressed in light of the quadrant each group is responsible for. It is helpful to stay loose and some-what playful with this step of the process, which relies heavily on creative, intuitive skills.

7. Examine Implications of Possible Decisions

Now it is time to test the original question against the various scenarios. In a world as described in this scenario, how would each response to this decision have played out? Is there a decision that would have played out well in all the scenarios? Are there vulnerabilities that a scenario has revealed that we could prepare for now? Remember, the purpose of a scenario is not to come up with one specific forecast of the future but rather to provide some thinking exercises for developing alternative contingencies.

8. Identify Leading Indicators and Signposts

The scenarios can be used to stimulate thinking before making the needed decision, but as time passes, you will begin to identify the scenario or parts of scenarios that are playing out closest to the actual course of history. At this point, it is helpful to identify some specific indicators or signposts that you can continue to monitor. Often, being able to spot these indicators will provide helpful clues and insights for further strategic thinking and decision-making.

Several approaches and methods of scenario planning are available, and the process lends itself to variation. The important thing to remember is that even if you do not follow the process precisely, an imaginative story that forces us to think and see the world in a new way can be a helpful outcome. In a period of rapidly accelerating change when long-term strategic planning may be a waste of time, scenario planning provides a means for congregations to think through not just one possible future but a variety of potential futures for which we can be better prepared.

Here is an example using the question of relocating the church from a downtown neighborhood to the growing sector of the city. Grace Church is located in a medium-size American city and was founded in the early 19th century. The church has a long and illustrious history; over the years it has had members serving in prominent positions in both the city and state governments. By the mid-1960s the church had grown to a membership of over 2,000 and had an average Sunday attendance of about 700. During the '70s Grace Church began to decline in average Sunday attendance as well as in programs and ministries. Much of this decline was a result of both businesses and residents relocating to the growing edge of the community. In 1976 the church purchased a parsonage in this growing area of the city.

The leadership at Grace Church discussed relocating the church to that neighborhood in the early 1980s but decided to stick it out and try to develop a different type of ministry to the downtown area. This ministry was never developed with any success. By 1996 Grace Church had steadily declined to an average Sunday attendance of 132.

From 1975 until 1996, one pastor led Grace Church faithfully. From his retirement until 1998 Grace Church employed a trained interim pastor, who conducted a major congregational study at Grace as well as extensive demographic research within a ten-mile radius of the church. Over the years, as attendance, programs, and ministries declined, Grace Church found itself with a substantial amount of unused space, so slowly the congregation began to lease it out to various agencies, including an independent day-care facility.

In 1996 a movement to redevelop the downtown area began in the riverfront area a few blocks from the church. Various shops and nightclubs opened. A major facility was erected on the river for a wide variety of public activities from concerts to ethnic food festivals.

Pastor Coulter arrived in time for the Christmas Eve service in 1998. She was recently married to a professional musician. A major developer had purchased and restored a row of Victorian houses adjacent to the street where the church is located. Pastor Coulter and her husband purchased one of the restored houses for their residence.

Before coming to Grace Church, Coulter was pastor for urban ministries at a large downtown parish in another city. In her former position she had initiated a successful ministry to the homeless and, with the help of her then fiancé (now her husband), had developed an alternative worship service on Saturday evenings that targeted people in their 20s and 30s. Before her ordination she had worked as a concert promoter and had even served a term as mayor of a moderate-size city on the east coast of Florida.

Shortly after Pastor Coulter's arrival, the judicatory approached Grace Church with the proposal to "partner" their resources and relocate the church beyond the growing edge of the city to an area that clearly would be thriving in the next three to five years. The judicatory felt that with the redevelopment of the riverfront area, this transition would offer an ideal time for Grace Church to get out and make a new start. With the sale of Grace Church's physical plant, the use of its endowments, and some assistance from the judicatory, Grace Church could build an attractive physical plant that would serve a congregation of 200 to 300 on five acres of land in the new area.

With an aging physical plant and church members feeling ambivalence and exhaustion from serving as a landlord to various tenants, the administrative board and even Pastor Coulter felt compelled to consider the offer. The decision would have to be made to relocate to the new location or to stay in the city and redevelop the existing remnant congregation. To make a decision the church would have to consider whether it was possible to develop a viable ministry in its current location.

Pastor Coulter gathered the administrative board and other key leaders in the congregation for a two-day retreat at a conference center. Earlier, she and the administrative board had contracted with a consultant to lead the scenario-planning process. The consultant helped the group narrow the question: If Grace Church remains in its current location, what would be the best way to redevelop its ministry to the evolving community? Several key factors were identified, including economic development in the neighborhood, continued restoration of unoccupied houses, opportunities for new ministry, diversity in the neighborhood and the congregation, and the potential for new lay leadership. The group agreed on two critical and uncertain driving forces: the continued level of migration out of the neighborhood and the degree of redevelopment of the riverfront area.

The two driving forces were depicted as two intersecting axes. The horizontal axis depicts the level of redevelopment in the neighborhood, and the vertical axis depicts the possible variance between an increasing and a decreasing migration from the downtown neighborhood. Each quadrant would provide guiding factors for a different story of how the neighborhood might evolve. Participants divided into four small groups with the assignment to write a story of how the neighborhood evolves in light of one of the quadrants.

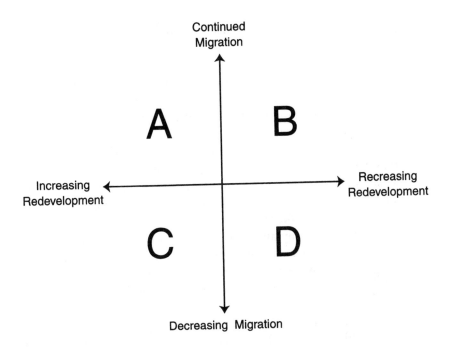

Story A: Continued increasing migration and increasing redevelopment. Over the next ten years the redevelopment project in the downtown area continued to develop, creating a major tourist attraction in the city. Many of the unoccupied houses were restored and converted into businesses such as antique shops and restaurants. Near the river a major hotel was built; eventually the city built a convention center. Activity and street traffic increased, with the area busy both day and night. There was increased pressure to push farther east up the river into what had historically been an African-American neighborhood. Two rows of houses were leveled to make room for a parking lot that would serve the convention center. The commercial development resulted in an increase in property taxes. The building that First Baptist Church formerly occupied was purchased and remodeled as a nightclub and concert hall.

Story B: Continued increasing migration and decreasing redevelopment. After several attempts and even with assistance from the city, the downtown riverfront redevelopment project was deemed a failure. A few of the nightclubs remained but drew activity only at night. The houses in the area became rentals, primarily to people in lower economic categories.

The increasing homeless population in the city frequented many of the abandoned houses and buildings.

Story C. Increased redevelopment and decreased migration. The downtown riverfront neighborhood flourished in the coming years. As more of the older, unoccupied houses were refurbished, a neighborhood organization was formed that began to organize to create some boundaries to the downtown commercial development. Younger couples began buying and restoring small bungalows on the edge of the historically African-American neighborhood. An unoccupied printing factory was converted into luxury loft apartments. An independent church bought the building that once housed First Baptist Church and began holding services. The commercial redevelopment remained primarily along the two streets that ran perpendicular to the river, while traditional neighborhood housing continued to be renovated for residential use. The old hospital building was converted into an assisted-care facility by a joint effort of several denominations.

Story D. Decreasing migration and decreasing redevelopment. Local housing stabilized as people began to choose to stay in the old neighborhood. The neighborhood evolved into about half owner-occupied dwellings and half rentals. The neighborhood population became relatively transient with the increase in rentals, mostly to students and Hispanic and Asian immigrants. A neighborhood watch was organized in an effort to keep the crime rate down. The local Southern Baptist Association used the building once occupied by First Baptist Church to launch a ministry to the immigrant community. A service in Spanish was held on Sunday mornings and a service in Korean in the evening.

Grace Church now asked, If it remained in the community, what would be the best way to redevelop its ministry to the evolving community? In light of the four stories, participants were able to envision several viable and useful ministries. In story A, they saw the need for a ministry of advocacy for the local residential neighborhood. In story B, parish leadership imagined buying and renovating some of the housing, or even one of the commercial properties to be used as a homeless shelter. In response to story C, the leadership could imagine an influx of new members into worship services from the thriving local neighborhood, as well as a ministry to the assisted-care facility. As the leaders considered the ramifications of story D, they realized that with such a transition, the congregation would have to make changes to reach out to its evolving local community. A diverse multicultural congregation with a variety of worship services was envisioned.

Although Grace Church could not predict which scenario would play out, its members could at least see the various possibilities for ministry in each story. Simply imagining the possibilities gave them the courage to decide to stay in their current location and refuse the judicatory proposal to relocate.

Scenario planning is more a tool for creative imagining than an exact planning process, but that innate flexibility makes it a helpful tool in a rapidly changing and unpredictable environment. The process provides not only a means of considering various perspectives on a question but also the opportunity for a group to imagine freely what God might do if we are obedient and willing to share a vision. The playful freedom of imagining scenarios gives the Holy Spirit the opportunity to work in our hearts and minds.

USING THE TOOLS

When I was a small boy, I used to spend considerable time with my maternal grandfather, who was a farmer. He had a respect for tools that was both appreciative and fearful. He took fastidious care of all his tools, from his John Deere tractor to screwdrivers and garden hoes. Everything was periodically cleaned and always stored in its proper place. Once he demonstrated to me the correct procedure to sharpen a garden hoe and then how to use the hoe. With ease and skill he gracefully slid the hoe under an intruding plant and cut it cleanly and smoothly at the roots. Then he said, "Son, that's what a hoe can do if you keep it sharp and learn to use it." Then he showed me the razor-sharp edge of the garden hoe and said, "Of course, if you're not careful and you don't know what you're doing, you can do a lot of damage with a tool." Years before he had lost the end of his thumb to an electric saw, and he now emphasized his point by running the nub of his thumb across the edge of the hoe.

Whether it is garden implements or methods of congregational development, tools can be dangerous. In the hands of people who are willing to learn and develop the appropriate skills, however, the tools I have described can help a congregation gain new perspective on its ministry. Even if a congregation has not thought of itself as a learning community, when these tools are used skillfully and consistently, congregational learning will take place.

1. Peter M. Senge, *The Fifth Discipline: The Art and Practice of the Learning Organization* (New York: Currency Doubleday, 1990), 4.

2. Senge, *Fifth Discipline,* 1.

3. Senge, *Fifth Discipline,* 2.

4. Senge, *Fifth Discipline,* 7.

5. Senge, *Fifth Discipline,* 141.

6. Esther de Waal, *Seeking God: The Way of St. Benedict* (Collegeville, Minn.: Liturgical Press, 1984), 69.

7. Senge, *Fifth Discipline,* 7.

8. Senge, *Fifth Discipline,* 142.

9. Senge, *Fifth Discipline,* 8.

10. Senge, *Fifth Discipline,* 9.

11. Senge, *Fifth Discipline,* 206.

12. Senge, *Fifth Discipline,* 207.

13. William Russell and T. Branch, *Second Wind: Memoirs of an Opinionated Man* (New York: Random House, 1979), quoted in Senge, *Fifth Discipline,* 233.

14. Senge, *Fifth Discipline,* 234-236.

15. Peter M. Senge, "Theory, Methods, & Tools," on-line database (Boston: Society for Organizational Learning, Massachusetts Institute of Technology, 1996), 3.

16. Virginia Anderson and Lauren Johnson, *Systems Thinking Basics: From Concepts to Causal Loops* (Cambridge, Mass: Pegasus Communications), 127.

17. Arlin J. Routhage, *Sizing Up a Congregation for New Member Ministry* (New York: Episcopal Church Center, 1982).

18. Anderson and Johnson, *Systems Thinking Basics,* 57.

19. David Cooperrider, Jane Magruder Watson, Diana Whitley, and Cathy Royal, *Appreciative Inquiry Consultant's Manual* (Washington: Jane Magruder Watson, 1996), 1.

20. Cooperrider, et al., *Appreciative Inquiry,* 3.

21. Cooperrider, et al., *Appreciative Inquiry,* 2.

22. Cooperrider, et al., *Appreciative Inquiry,* preface.

23. David Bohm, Donald Factor, and Peter Garrett, "Dialogue: A Proposal," self-published on the Internet, 1991 (www.world.std.com/"lo/bohm/0001.html).

24. Cooperrider, et al., *Appreciative Inquiry,* 21.

25. John P. Kotter, *Leading Change* (Boston: Harvard Business School Press, 1996), 145-147.

26. Edgar H. Schein, *Organizational Culture and Leadership* (San Francisco: Jossey-Bass, 1992), 16.

27. Schein, *Organizational Culture,* 17.

28. Schein, *Organizational Culture,* 22.

29. Schein, *Organizational Culture,* 26.

30. Schein, *Organizational Culture,* 152.

31. Peter Schwartz, "Using Scenarios," accessed on-line (Emeryville, Calif: Global Business Networks, 1997),1 (www.gbn.org/).

32. Peter Schwartz, *The Art of the Long View: Planning for the Future in an Uncertain World* (New York: Currency Doubleday, 1991), 3-4.

33. Schwartz, *Art of the Long View,* 8.

34. Schwartz, *Art of the Long View,* 241.

35. Gill Ringland, *Scenario Planning: Managing for the Future* (London: John Wiley & Sons, 1998), 229.

36. Schwartz, *Art of the Long View,* 243.

*W*elcome to the work of Alban Institute...
the leading publisher and congregational resource organization for clergy and laity today.

Your purchase of this book means you have an interest in the kinds of information, research, consulting, networking opportunities and educational seminars that Alban Institute produces and provides. We are a non-denominational, non-profit 25-year-old membership organization dedicated to providing practical and useful support to religious congregations and those who participate in and lead them.

Alban is acknowledged as a pioneer in learning and teaching on *Conflict Management *Faith and Money *Congregational Growth and Change *Leadership Development *Mission and Planning *Clergy Recruitment and Training *Clergy Support, Self-Care and Transition *Spirituality and Faith Development *Congregational Security.

Our membership is comprised of over 8,000 clergy, lay leaders, congregations and institutions who benefit from:
- ❖ 15% discount on hundreds of Alban books
- ❖ $50 per-course tuition discount on education seminars
- ❖ Subscription to *Congregations*, the Alban journal (a $30 value)
- ❖ Access to Alban research and (soon) the "Members-Only" archival section of our web site www.alban.org

For more information on Alban membership or to be added to our catalog mailing list, call 1-800-486-1318, ext.243 or return this form.

Name and Title: _____

Congregation/Organization: _____

Address: _____

City: _____ Tel.: _____

State: _____ Zip: _____ Email: _____

BKIN

The Alban Institute
ATTN: MEMBERSHIP
7315 Wisconsin Avenue
Suite 1250 West
Bethesda, MD 20814-3211

Stamp
Here